SOUND ORIGINS

DEVELOPING YOUR MUSICAL IDENTITY

FOR MUSICIANS, COMPOSERS, & EDUCATORS

Copyright © 2014 Jim Robitaille Music

ISBN-13: 978-0692492437

ISBN-10: 0692492437

All rights reserved. No part of this book may be reproduced, stored in a retrieval system, or transmitted in any form or by any means, electronic, mechanical, photocopying, recording, scanning, or otherwise, without the prior written permission of the publisher, except for the inclusion of brief quotations embodied in critical reviews. For information contact info@jimrobitaille.com

Disclaimer

All the material contained in this book is provided for educational and informational purposes only. While every attempt has been made to provide information that is both accurate and effective, the author does not assume any responsibility for the accuracy or use/misuse of this information.

Prerequisite

Some of the examples, exercises and concepts presented in this book assume a basic knowledge of your instrument, music fundamentals, theory, harmony and technique. That being said, this book is truly intended for musicians on all levels, and can continue to be applied as each person advances with their own musical studies. To purchase optional MP3 audio and score files for Sound Origins go to www.jimrobitaille.com/store

Acknowledgments

I would like to recognize and dedicate this book to the teachers, musicians, students, and listeners who I have had the honor to learn, play, and share music with through the years. These are the sources and channels that have essentially influenced and help shape many of the ideas presented in this publication.

I would like to thank author William Powers for his initial interest, time, and very helpful insights along the way. I wish to express my gratitude to Elizabeth Aldred for her excellent and thorough help with the book's copy editing and structural content. A very special thanks to Bruce Abbott for his all out true friendship, effective ideas, guidance, and generous help with editing and test driving some of the concepts in this book in his own creative and musical way.

I would like to also thank D'Addario Strings and Planet Waves for their continued support and fantastic products.

Cover Art

Oksana Lubianova

Lastly, I would like to thank you for your purchase of this book. Your support is greatly appreciated. May it be a helpful and inspirational guide for you and your music.

Jim Robitaille 2014

Table of Contents

Introduction 5

Chapter 1 The Micro Steps To Sound Creation 7
    Intent 7
    Intention Example. Slow Tuesday 9
    Touch 10
    Attack 11
    Sound and Timbre 12
    Technique 13
    Articulation 14
    Articulation Names and Symbols 16
    Dynamics 17
    Dynamic Examples 19
    Ornamentation 19
    Ornamentation Names and Symbols 21
    Ornamentation Example 22
    Expression 22
    Tempo designations 23
    Style and Mood Designations 23
    Rhythm 24
    Phrasing 29
    Jazz Phrasing Example 30
    Nuance and Inflection 30
    Nuance Inflection Example 32

Chapter 2 Transcription 35
    Learning Solos Without Transcription 38
    Learning Solos With Transcription 39
    Transcription Rhythm Examples 40
    Transcription Pitch Example 41
    Transcribing Without an Instrument 42
    Solo Analysis 42

Chapter 3 Composition 44
    Exercise 1. Beginning the History of Your Composition 45
    Exercise 1. Composition Examples 47
    Exercise 2. Composing with Modes 48
    Exercise 2. Composition Examples 50
    Exercise 3. Composing With One Chord Quality and Motif 51
    Composition Example 3. Back To Bayeux 53
    Exercise 4. Composing using a Jazz Contrafact 54
    Composition Example 4: Lost And Found 55

Chapter 4 Arranging 56
    *Yesterdays – Jerome Kern 56

Chapter 5 Improvisation 58

Chapter 6 The Art of Listening 64

Chapter 7 Other Art Forms 66
    Visual Arts 66
    Visual Arts Example: Figures 67
    Poetry 68
    Literature 69
    Literature Example: Arthur C 70
    Nature 73

Chapter 8 Travel and Other Cultures 74

Chapter 9 Internal Health. Energy, Essence and Spirit 76
    Jing or Essence of Life. 76
    Qi or Chi. Energy of Life, Breath, Air. 77
    Shen. The Spirit of Life 77

Chapter 10 The Instrument & Equipment - The Machine 79

Chapter 11 Overview And Summary 81

Afterword 85

Song Title Discography 86

About The Author 87

Introduction

"Because of this, originality consists of returning to the origin."
– Antonio Gaudi

In our desire to know and become aware of our own sound and style in music many of us are often directed to look to means outside of ourselves. Although there are many important channels and resources available for us to explore and learn from such as recordings, books, videos, live performances, lessons, classes and so forth, we can easily overlook the desired natural sound that is lying there within us ready to be tapped.

Here are a couple of analogies to help illustrate this point.

Let's take the cat or kitten that chases its own tail in perpetual circles. The cat, never catching up with the tail, possibly thinking the tail is something else detached from itself to chase like a mouse, eventually gives up and collapses in exhaustion. (Great entertainment for us by the way), not so sure how the cat may feel about it.

When we learn to speak our parents' language or languages, we immediately assume our own speaking voice as it is developed over time through imitation, learning, living and assimilation. We never question it, and actually never really even try to develop it in most cases. Although we learn so much from our own life experience in the world that influences and shapes our person to some degree, we ultimately end up being and sounding like ourselves. We are usually not even aware of how we sound to our own ears until we hear our voice for the first time on a voice mail message or a recording, from the outside in. This is sometimes accompanied by the realization that we may not even like how we sound, and are in disbelief that it is even our own voice that we are hearing on the recording. In time we learn to accept the way we sound, and grow to like it, at least to some extent. And so the cat eventually comes to terms with the fact that its tail was attached all along, and our own voice developed independently of the many external sources and influences from our early years.

As we move through the content that is covered in this book, we will explore many areas both in and out of music that will allow us to learn more about ourselves, what we are drawn to, and how we can develop and bring this into our own musical vision and sound.

Chapter 1 The Micro Steps To Sound Creation

When thinking about sound we might hear it in a whole, or macro way as just one thing. In this chapter I will break it down so we can become aware of what the sound's more immediate micro aspects are, as well as to where this leads us with the other crucial areas that inform our playing after the sound is put forth. As we move through the first chapter, try and think about how you approach each one of these steps in your music.

Intent

Before we even make a sound there is hopefully some kind of purpose and intention behind it.

In music this can mean many things depending on the situation, and on what we *intend* on doing or saying in the music. The intention can be, and usually is, driven by our emotional and feeling state with the music at that moment, even if it just begins with something as simple as what the title of the tune means to us. The content of our intention can be stimulated by the pure sound and interplay from any band member, or our physical relationship to our own instrument, how we approach playing it, and how we evolve in transcending it at times. Do we hear anything before we play? Do we play what we hear? What was the meaning of what we just played in relation to the music? As with any language, we hope our communicative output in music is informed by what we aim for and intend to say.

Even though intent is not an actual physical part of the sound, I feel it is important to speak about this here, since it both leads to and informs the content of the sound in our ideas and how we develop them. Just as with spoken language or a lyric, it is equally important with our intention to be coherent when we begin to say something on our chosen instrument in the world of musical syntax.

The following example is the second verse of the first section of a composition I wrote, to which I added lyrics later on. Here we can see how the above spoken language analogy can apply to a melody and lyric in the way they come together and share a union with the rhythm, phrase length, melodic contour, inflection, and in this example, the abstract poetry of the lyrics. You could also try this out with another song if you desire.

Slow Tuesday 2nd Verse Lyric Excerpt by Jim Robitaille

Just as daybreak waits for twilight's dawn

into darkness for a while

stars fall out into another world that never fades

in its own time slow Tuesday

Intention Example. Slow Tuesday

Slow Tuesday

Concert Key

Jim Robitaille

A

F#m9(omit3) — Db/F — Em(b6) — Eb7SUS Abm7
Just as day-break waits for twi-light's

DMA7 — AMA7 — G#7(#5) — C#7(b9)
dawn in-to dark-ness for a while

F#m(omit3) — Db/F — E — Eb7(#9) Eb7(b9)
stars fall out in-to a-no-ther world that ne-ver

DMA7 — Ebm11 C#m11 — G#(omit3) B(omit3) — C#m(omit3)
fades in its own time slow Tues-day

© 1994 Jim Robitaille Music

Touch

I like to think of touch as the inception to sound. Touch is the first thing that takes place right before the attack begins and the sound actually takes place. By paying special attention to the details of touch we can learn a lot about how we play in respect to both the good and bad habits that can be nurtured and corrected.

Put on a recording of any great musician and listen for their touch. For example: Ella Fitzgerald's voice, Bill Evan's piano, Kenny Wheeler, Wes Montgomery, João Gilberto, Wayne Shorter, Charlie Haden, Roswell Rudd, Charlie Parker, Billy Higgins, and so many others, and their intrinsic qualities that may speak to you. Vladimir Horowitz, one of the greatest pianists of the twentieth century, was of the Russian school of piano which taught that the sound came from the whole body starting from the toes.

Touch is an extremely important aspect of the sound that we pick up on when listening to someone on their instrument. Slow practice and attention to details in positioning, and again, our intent, can develop good practice habits and a desired touch for us. A great way to incorporate this is when you slowly practice new lines or scales.

Listen to just the touch of the musicians you like on your instrument first, then gravitate to other instrumentalists and graft from them. A live performance is one of the best way to witness this. You could transcribe and analyze other musicians just for the touch of each note or phrase. Touch is one of the most important and personal elements of sound reproduction so be sure to give it special attention when you practice and play.

Attack

The attack of the note follows the touch. Touch and attack are so closely related to each other in the time and space in which they occur that they can seem as one, which in the big macro picture they are.

Attack triggers the *vibration* that sets the sound of the instrument into motion. Attack comes in many forms, and at times we are required to use certain attacks to convey the specific music at hand. At other times, especially as improvisers, we have the freedom to express what is coming through us with any type of attack we may want to use. How we dig in or lay back, by accenting or not as we respond to the music, is dictated by our attack. Being aware of over-attacking at times is also important, since at some threshold point the notes will not get any louder and will actually cancel themselves out to some degree, as is the case with plucked string instruments.

The attack can bring out the beauty and extreme tonal properties of the instrument and is a great approach to exploiting the beautiful sounds that each instrument has to offer. So as an exercise, spend some time listening analytically to recordings of yourself and to others for the attack of notes after the initial touch takes place. Notice what you like and what you don't like. What would you want to hear there? How would your attack be different? Later on in this chapter we will discuss articulation, which offers us various ways to deliver our attack.

Sound and Timbre

After the initial attack we hear the sound of the notes played. We experience the very sound nature and vibration of the instrument along with its tone quality or timbre, craftsmanship, and many other aspects depending on the type of instrument it is. Some instruments give you nothing at all in the way of sound until you develop some technique on them, like brass, woodwind and double reed instruments. Other instruments give you some sort of a sound even if you cannot play them very well, like piano, some string instruments, and the voice. I say this because guitarists for instance, sometimes take for granted how much sound the instrument offers without much attention early on to the details of touch, tone, and sound reproduction from their own hands. However, a saxophonist cannot even show up to play without committing a substantial amount of time and effort towards developing a sound.

All instruments have their challenges and limitations, and there can be much to learn and to understand in what others go through to just produce a basic sound on their instrument. It goes without saying that a certain amount of technique is needed to produce, support, and sustain a good sound and intonation on the various instruments we play.

Emulation of the players, composers, and singers you admire is part of the process of experiencing, learning, and reproducing what you like in their sound and music. This will help you to assimilate new vocabulary, ideas, and techniques that will gradually become a part of your own emerging sound expression.

How do you sound on your chosen instrument? Have you outgrown it, or is there still a lot of room for development on your part to bring out the best in what you want to hear in, and out of yourself? Is there balance in the lower, middle and upper registers in reference to frequency and volume? Is the sound too dark, too bright, too harsh, too small, or is it warm, brilliant, rich, full and big? What do you like and prefer when you listen to players and singers? Again, what do you hear, or you want to hear in your own sound?

It is very important to remember that the sound of your instrument is the first thing you project outward to the listener and one of the main elements they will take away from a performance.

Listen to players on your chosen instrument and take note of what appeals to you in their sound. Also listen to all instrumentalists and singers for what stands out to you and what you can learn and incorporate in your own way into your sound and timbre.

In closing this section, I would also like to mention the innovations throughout the years with synthesis in electronic sound creation. The study and experimentation in psychoacoustics (the study of the psychological and physiological perceptions of sound in music), have furthered and stretched the boundaries of instrumental timbre by including many new hybrids and tone colors with endless combinations of instruments and elements that can fire the imagination and open your mind even further into sound creation. There are many expressive synthesizer solos that have inspired me over the years from Joe Zawinul, Jan Hammer, Chick Corea, and Herbie Hancock to name a few.

Technique

As mentioned in the previous section, a certain amount of technique is needed to even produce a sound on certain instruments. In the end, we can say that technique is the ability acquired to be able to express whatever we may need or want to say at any moment with our instrument and sound. It is the delivery system.

Just as when we speak, we are focused on what we want to say at any moment, and the skills or techniques acquired through time to effectively express ourselves become an involuntary intuitive act for us.

An instrument or voice in many ways is like a machine that we have to learn to operate to an end as an extension of ourselves, so we can express our innermost feelings through it into the music. Years of assimilated training and repetition are required to achieve various levels of knowledge and skill to arrive at a *technique* on the instrument. Because it is obviously assumed by students that a lot has to be learned to execute what they want to play, time to achieve everything is a given, and with all of this sometimes comes two important areas to be aware of and balance out amongst less experienced players. The individuals who may have enough technique to express themselves, but may need to learn other musical skills and mature towards a more complete expression in their music. Others may be under prepared regarding their own technique, and are limited in this area even though they may be able to hear most of what they want to express and are innately musical.

Acquiring and maintaining technique is a must, and it needs to be developed and become strong enough to support your sound and the music you want to convey. Knowing what is needed to express yourself, and the way you hear and want to play, will point you in the direction of the techniques you need to deliver the music in your own way.

The most important thing in the end is how you use your technique at any given moment, which will hopefully be just what you need to it be, in sound and in respect to the music at hand.

Articulation

How the notes are played in reference to their attack and length in comparison to one another creates the articulation. There are many articulation techniques that are achieved a number of ways on many different string, woodwind, brass, keyboard and percussion instruments. Take note of the ones you already use both consciously and unconsciously in your playing and incorporate the others that are new or not utilized as often.

There are many articulations that exist to support all the music that has been created throughout history. Some articulation techniques pertain to specific instruments only, and it would be beyond the purpose of this book to list every one.

Take the time to listen to other types of music outside of what you choose and want to play most of the time. Various musical dialects will have many different intrinsic qualities, techniques, rhythms, harmonies, and articulations, to express the specific musical needs of that style. Some of these can have a great impact and influence on how we may use articulation with our own playing.

Articulation is one of the most important aspects of what makes many great musicians sound unique with their own idiosyncratic approach to how they play the notes. Find the articulations that naturally speak to you, and that you gravitate towards, and incorporate them into your song melodies and improvisations.

Here is a short list of some articulation names and symbols that will affect notes in sustained, short, long, accented, connected, and dampened ways.

Articulation Names and Symbols

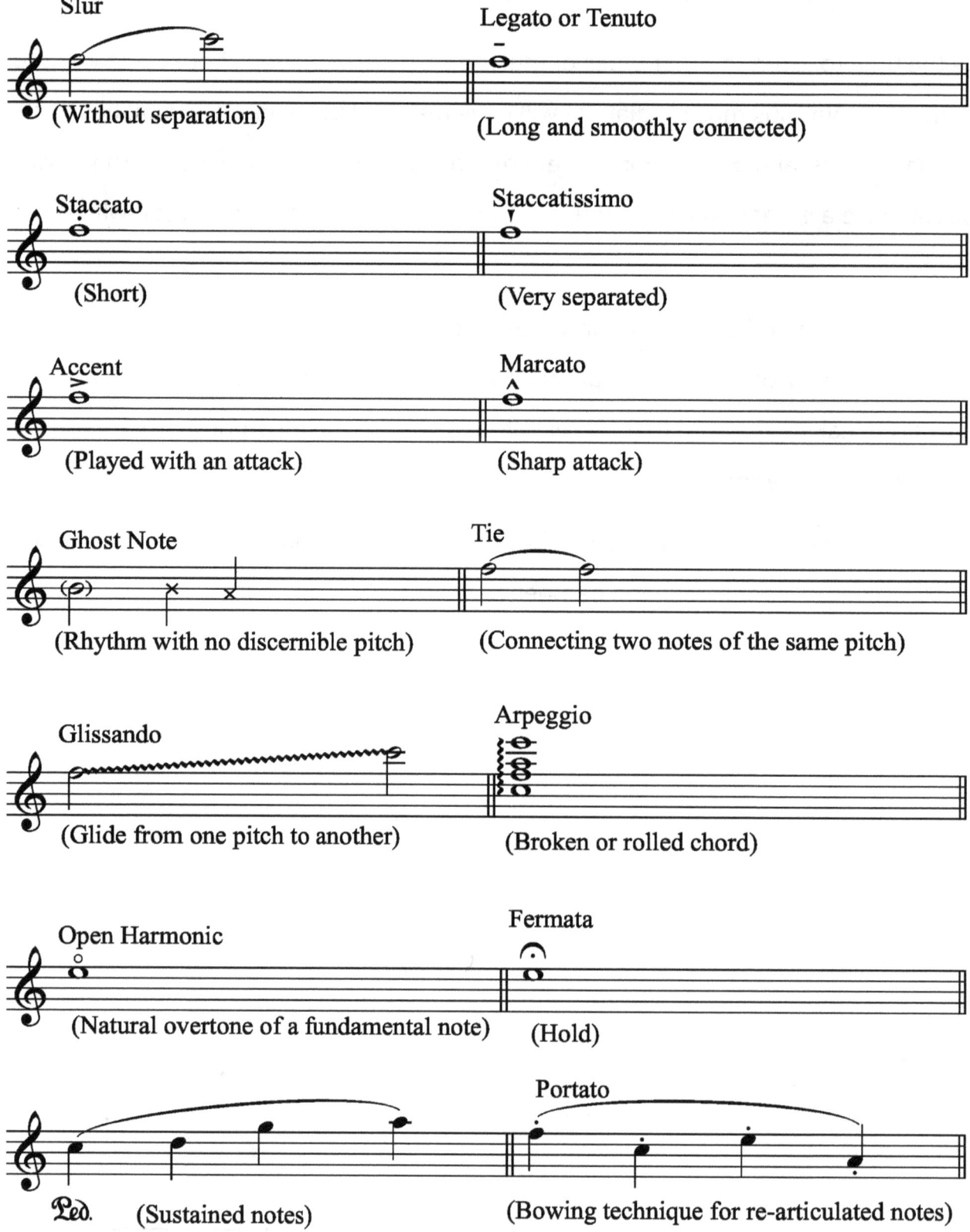

Dynamics

Dynamics dictate the relative volume between the notes or an entire piece of music. The dynamic level of music is what breathes life into it, from both a compositional and performance standpoint. We use dynamics when we speak to emphasize what we are saying or to fit the situation, like whispering at the library or shouting out at the peaceful protest. We can bring the listeners in closer to us by playing softer, or come to them with higher volumes.

The innovative jazz guitarist Jim Hall used to turn the volume of his guitar all the way off midway through a chordal passage, and then turn it back up again, creating a very musical and dramatic dynamic soundscape within the music.

In a group context it is imperative that each individual be able to understand how to perform and respond with the full range of dynamics that is needed for the music at anytime.

Some of the basic dynamics markings and their relative interpretation in music include:

- *pp* – pianissimo. Very soft
- *p* – piano. Soft
- *mp* – mezzo piano. Moderately soft
- *mf* – mezzo forte. Moderately loud
- *f* – forte. Loud
- *ff* – forte. Very loud
- *sfz* – sforzando. Loud and accented
- ⟨ – crescendo. Becoming louder
- ⟩ – decrescendo or diminuendo. Becoming softer
- Calmando – calm

- Morendo – dying away, also tempo change

Of course some of these dynamic symbols can be extended in many instances if needed.

As musicians, we are the first listeners on the bandstand, and need to have a wide auditory awareness of where each performer is in reference to the dynamic level for the music to unfold desirably. Dynamics can bring a life and vibrancy to your art by expressing strong emotional elements in ways that could not otherwise be delivered to the listener. When you listen to music, observe the dynamic changes in the music and the result this has. The presence of dynamics can keep our listening senses alert to the music as opposed to shutting them down when the whole piece and the various instruments are being played at an unchanging volume level.

Improvisors can practice changing the dynamic level from soft to loud or loud to soft within a phrase, or by alternating every other phrase when improvising on a tune. You can also control the whole dynamic curve of an entire chorus of a solo by thinking bigger as opposed to just phrase by phrase. With the inclusion of dynamics, you can learn a whole lot about how to control your instrument in reference to your technique, while at the same time breathing new life into your playing, singing and writing.

Dynamic Examples

"Adagio" Excerpt by Jim Robitaille
Ex.1

Ex. 2 "Adagio" Bridge excerpt

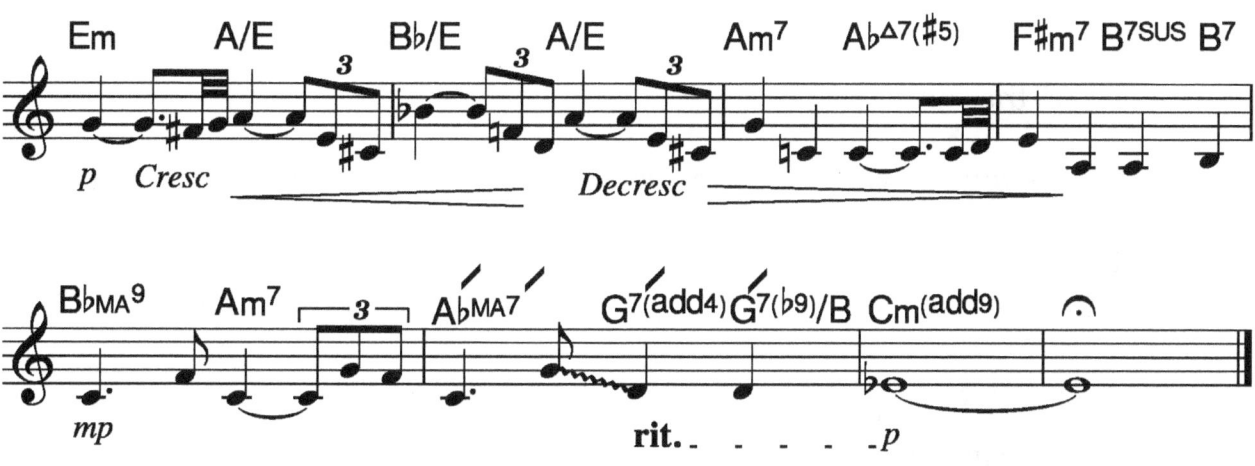

Ornamentation

Ornamental flourishes in music are at many times optional and interpreted by the performer depending on the situation and historical period of music. The exploitation of ornaments in music has been extremely important and is a necessary addition in personalizing a unique expression with melody, harmony, and rhythm for composers, instrumentalists, and vocalists. This has a great effect on the vocabulary and idiosyncrasies of musicians, and how it all comes across in what they are saying.

Listen to how players utilize ornamentation at the start of their lines, as well as within, and especially at the end of phrases.

Ornamentations have different results and effects in the many styles of music they are used in. It can be very helpful to incorporate these not only in your song melodies and improvisations, but also in the exercises and etudes you may practice and warm up with in other styles. Listen for them, and get to know how to recognize them and to make use of them.

As an exercise, create and write out a two to eight bar line from a song you like to play on or sing, or from one of your original compositions. Play the line you've written out and repeat it with each of the ornamental devices from the examples listed, utilizing them in different parts of the line that seem to work best with how you hear them. You can also use various combinations of ornamentation in the line as well.

As you familiarize yourself with practicing and using these ornamentations, you will start to hear them more naturally when you play, sing or write. There are many other ornaments as well like dampened notes and vibrato. You can make use of those too if you want.

Here are some common ornamentations.

Ornamentation Names and Symbols

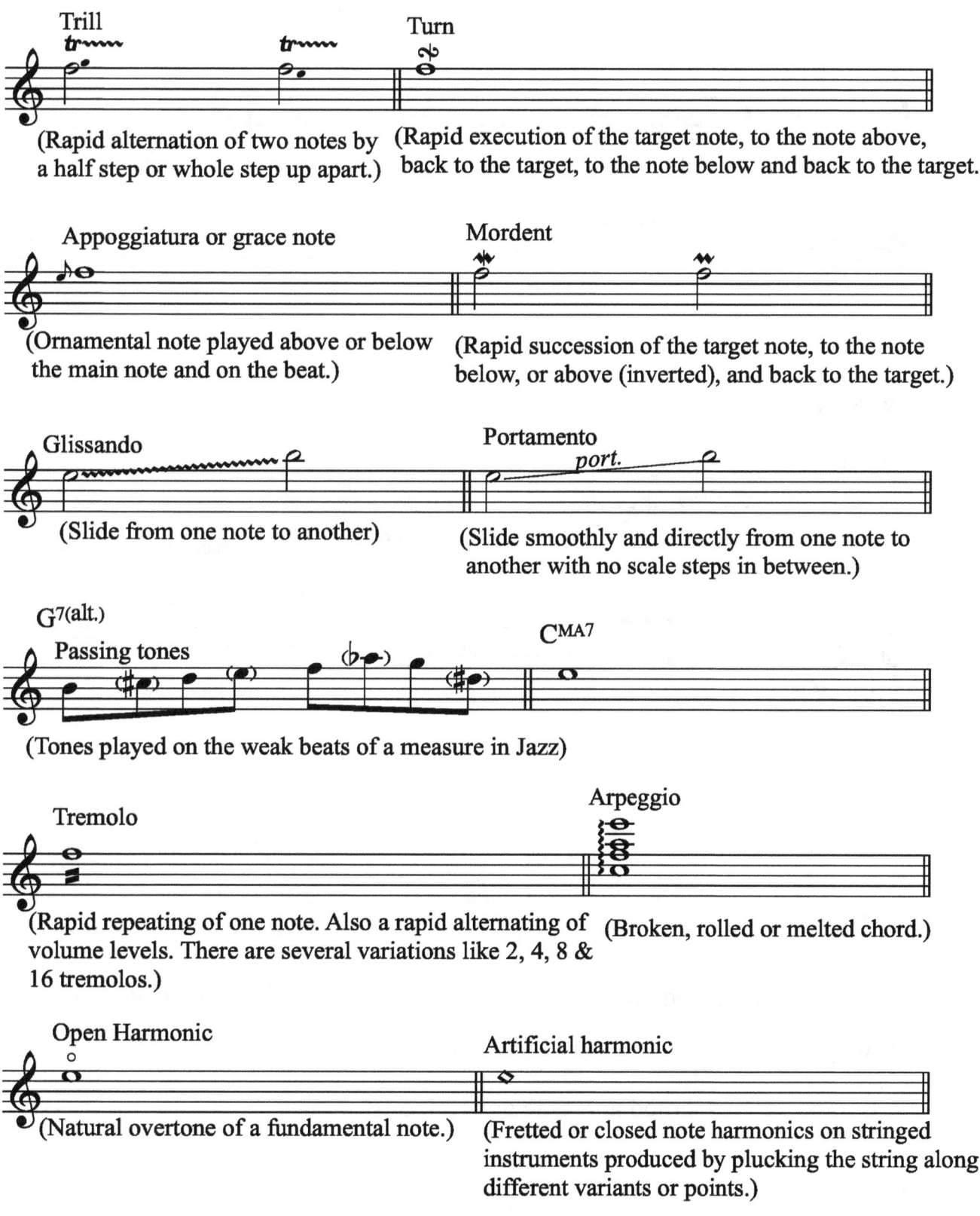

Ornamentation Example

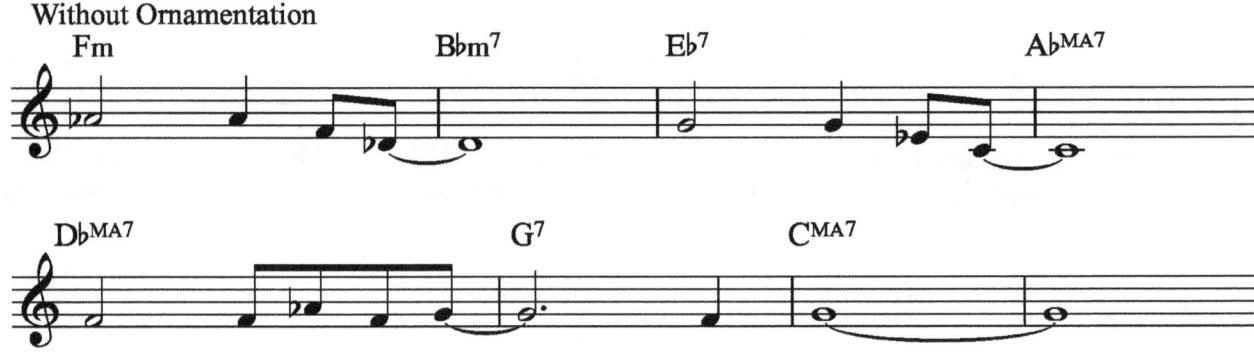

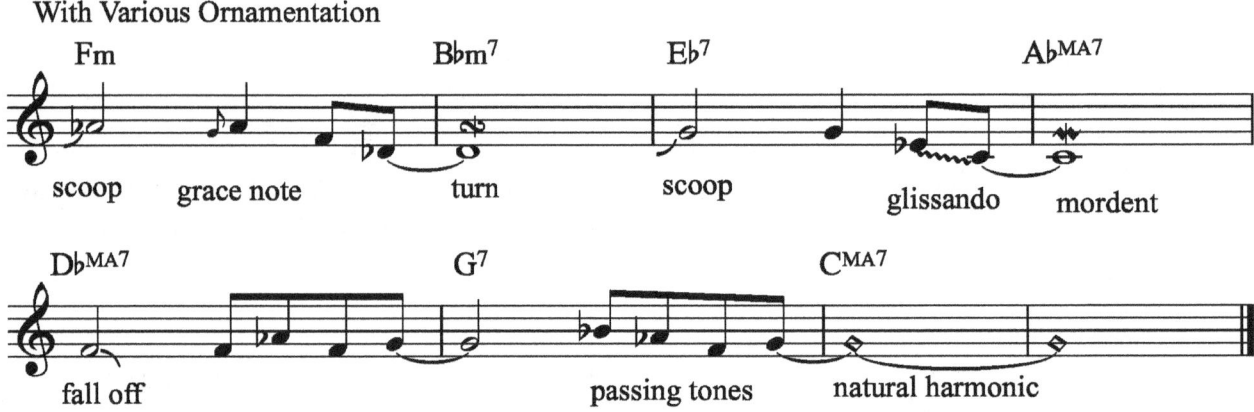

Expression

Expression markings sometimes refer to all of the previously mentioned elements. More specifically they typically refer to tempo and its variations in style and mood.

Here are some various tempo and style designations in music:

Tempo designations

- Largo – slow, broad and dignified
- Adagio - slow
- Andante – moderately slow
- Moderato - moderate in speed
- Allegro – moderately fast
- Presto – very fast
- Ritardando – slowing down
- Rubato – played freely

Style and Mood Designations

- Con Brio – lively, with vigor
- Animato - played animated
- Espressivo – expressively
- Maestoso - majestic and stately
- Misterioso – with mystery, secretive

When we improvise or compose music, we can keep these expression designations in mind to be more in accord with the music and feeling of the moment. This is very powerful, and will bring as much meaning to our playing and writing as any other musical attribute we use.

A great exercise for this is to improvise on, or write a tune using some of these expression designations. This is great for the imagination.

Jazz pianist and composer Thelonious Monk composed and titled one of his compositions with the last expression element on the list, "Misterioso".

Rhythm

Rhythm is in everything. It is in our walk and in our talk. It is in the ocean tides, the movement of the wind, the birds' song or call, the earth's rotation, our entire biology, its blood flow and its breath. I have even seen it exist in an amazingly joyous musical ritual with some African cultures while they take part in the basic communal chore of doing the laundry.

Rhythm is the most common and basic of the sound dimensions in music, and no instrument can produce without it.

In one sense we are all drummers, generating and projecting the rhythmic output of our instruments into motion and into the air.

No matter how beautiful or hip a melody that we play may be, it will not be very effective at all if it is not informed by a strong coherent rhythm behind it. Even music expressed freely or in rubato time still needs its own sense of pacing and inner rhythm that clearly defines one musical phrase into the next.

The source of rhythm has a universal evolution throughout all nature and time itself.

The march rhythm goes back as far as Chopin, Mozart and Beethoven who incorporated it into their works and operas. Over the course of a few hundred years marches came to the shores of the United States, and the military marches were transformed and influenced by the syncopated rhythms brought into play by both the free and enslaved African presence. This rhythmic transformation helped develop and empower many roots of American jazz through work songs, call and response, gospel, blues, syncopated brass bands, ragtime and so forth.

I would urge you to acquire an overview of the numerous rhythmic dialects and how they have influenced and developed the music and dance of various cultures over time, and how they can enrich your own rhythmic ideas. Take the time to seek out and listen to the vast history of music from many regions and cultures around the world.

Here are some examples.

- The music of the Baltic states along with central, eastern and southeastern Europe stretches as far back as the medieval period up through to the orchestral, folkloric, and Slavic traditions found in Poland, Bulgaria, Hungary, and dozens of other countries. The music of Bulgaria and Hungary is highly advanced rhythmically as is evident in their folk music as in the Bulgarian State Woman's Choir.

- Russia is in northern Eurasia and is the largest country in the world. It has contributed some very important art, folk and popular music from several of the greatest composers throughout history such as Tchaikovsky, Prokofiev, and Shostakovich. Igor Stravinsky contributed some of the most advanced multi-metric music with his ballet The Rite of Spring.

- The numerous periods of western European orchestral, chamber and folk music traditions have been some of the most beloved and time-tested music of the western world for hundreds of years. From Early music to the present day, centuries of music are still performed that were created by some of the most important composers in history including Bach, Mozart, Ravel, Beethoven, Mahler, Haydn, Handle, Strauss, Schumann, and Debussy.

- The Islands of Great Britain and the Celtic music of Ireland and Scotland are very popular in many parts of the world through their traditional and modern popular music innovations.

- There is great traditional, orchestral and modern music from the Nordic lands of Iceland, Sweden, Finland (Sibelius), Norway (Grieg), and Denmark (Nielsen), which have also been a home for pop music, folkloric music, and some very important and innovative Nordic improvisors for decades.

- Listen to the abundant history of North American music including: the Aboriginal, pop, and jazz music from Canada. Greenland, the largest island in the world has music that draws on influences from both sides of the Atlantic Ocean as well as having many Arctic origins. Mexico has its rich folkloric musical history reaching to the Yucatan Peninsula along with a significant contribution to popular song. The isthmus of Central America is home to seven different countries with many artists having contributed to a great musical legacy through a divergent array of Latin jazz influences and musical hybrids. Also check out the great music of the Appalachian Mountains, and the several derivatives of funk that evolved along the East Coast of the U.S. We have the various dialects of the blues, and the dozens of great composers and music from Tin Pan Alley and American popular song. There is bluegrass, country, folk music, spirituals, gospel, ragtime, Creole music, and the many decades and innovations of jazz that brought us numerous innovative musicians, composers, rhythms, and music.

  Sam Lightning Hopkins was probably one of the first solo self-accompanied blues guitarists whose contributions were an important part of the early history of solo jazz guitar.

- The music of the West Indies includes soca, calypso, reggae, bachata, merengue to name a few, along with the origins of the steel pan drums from Trinidad. Much of the language and music is a blend of tradition and demographics, along with French, African, and Spanish influences. Close by to all of this we have the very important music of Cuba and Puerto Rico which has influenced and shaped innovations in Latin jazz and popular music in the United States and beyond for many years.

- The vast musical traditions and rhythms of South America include Brazil's numerous rhythmic dialects from the Northeastern states down through the Costa Verde, especially the bossa nova, samba, afoxe, choro, baião rhythms, and many more. There is also Argentina, home of the traditional tango and new tango, and the beautiful indigenous mountain music and contemporary music of Chile, Ecuador, Uruguay, Colombia and Peru. All of these countries and their culture are unique and have been extremely contributive in regards to rhythm and music in the world.

- The music and many regions of India, especially the highly enlightened and advanced musical tradition of the raga, embrace both the classical and improvisational traditions in one type of music. The art of south Indian konnakol and tala are combined in a highly advanced system of rhythm and syllables which has been the primary source of study for many musicians in the development of metric modulation in western music and improvisation. The inclusion of micro-tonal notes and scales in Indian music embrace a language that is more linear in approach in contrast to the harmonic vocabulary used in western music.

- Micro-tones are also found in the music of Indonesia more commonly found in Bali, Java, and Sumatra. The popular gamelan ensembles and the many improvisational and instrumental ensembles offer an ear into another world of exotic music, instrumentation, percussion, and culture.

- The countries of the Middle or Near East, present very old traditions and incredible musical offerings and instrumentation to the world with the musical cultures and rhythms of Lebanon, Armenia, Pakistan, Egypt, Israel, and several others. I have several recordings I like by the oud player Anouar Brahem. Although from Tunis, Tunisia in North Africa, you will hear the cultural and regional influences in his music.

- Spain has had a very important and long musical history and tradition. The highly rhythmic flamenco music which originated in the south, has existed from the 15th century along with the numerous periods of classical guitar literature to the present day, and the great history of orchestral composers and their musical contributions. Some of this music has also had a significant influence on Latin American music. The many regions of the country, such as the Iberian Peninsula, have been influenced by a diverse cultural array of music from its neighbors like the Middle East. The music in the northwest reaches as far back as the middle ages and is also home to the gaita, a Spanish version of the bagpipe.

- The music of eastern and southeast Asia includes the seemingly limitless musical history and instruments from: Japan, China, Mongolia, Korea, Russia, Vietnam, Cambodia, Burma, Singapore, Thailand, the Philippines and more.

- Oceania and Polynesia represent thousands of islands including New Zealand, Hawaii, New Guinea (the second largest island in the world in Melanesia), and the continent of Australia which has gifted us with several unique musical instruments like the bullroarer, didgeridoo, and the gum-leaf which were born out of the ancestry and traditions of its Aboriginal people.

- It is evident and documented that our genetic code and the European migration stem from the continent of Africa. The native, traditional, and modern African music, and its influence on so much of the world's musical traditions support this, and show musically what the African continent and its diaspora have offered to us all for so long. There is so much tribal and modern music from the southern, northern, eastern, western and central regions of Africa to explore and open our minds, hearts, and ears to.

Phrasing

Phrasing is so vast an area that it really embraces all the aforementioned aspects present in how we express and apply our sound and ideas. Getting as comfortable with expressing various short, medium, and long phrases, as we do in our spoken language, will expand and open up our ability to state our ideas in more creative ways as with asymmetrical phrasing for example.

The rest or silence that takes place between the phrases is equally important. How musicians pace and take their time with each element of the rhythm, melody, or harmony, reveals their own internal connection with that moment in the music. It also allows for the time to reflect on what was just played and heard, and to respond to it in a continuum.

One aspect of phrasing deals with the variables between players in regards to the way they convey rhythm with their own personal time feel. We typically learn to play in the center of the beat early on. In other styles we also learn to play ahead of the beat (much in the way Brazilian melodies are phrased sometimes, as with singer João Gilberto,) or behind the beat and stretching the time in jazz and blues as with singer Betty Carter.

For the most part, this playing behind or ahead of the beat is an effect that is used to create the desired tension or emotional feeling in response to the music. Working with a metronome, and a lot of listening and playing to recordings, can instill a natural sense of these time attributes so we can react and have them present in our own rhythmic systems and playing.

Another area that affects our phraseology in music deals with the numerous techniques and articulations available to each instrumentalist, and how they are applied to melodic lines. Jazz or swing phraseology has a triplet feeling in the eighth notes with the first note played long and the second note of the grouping played short along with a varied ratio of time between the first and second notes depending on the tempo. Try the following phrasing example at various tempos adjusting the articulation and narrowing the swing ratio between the eighth notes as you increase the tempo.

Jazz Phrasing Example

With all this, the internal editing, knowledge, and theory are working in the background as in any other language we have become adept at, with what we want to say and express being in the forefront.

Nuance and Inflection

Another important area in its own right after the sound is put forth is *Nuance*. Nuance represents the subtleties of expression in how melodies and chords are played, but are not usually notated in most cases. The way we approach both coming into and out of our notes and phrases affecting their color and tone is very personal. It can consist of effects not unlike what a painter may use, like smearing or blurring elements on the canvas, or for us, the notes on the auditory canvas. All instrumentalists can express some of these nuances, as well as having unique sets of their own from very subtle to extreme, depending on their instrument and the nature and style of the music being played. This is a great way to discover your internal response to feelings, expression, and the adventurous and explorative side to your personality.

Inflection in language typically affects the rise and fall of tone, and pitch.

Try the following phrases and observe how they sound when spoken in regards to the changes in volume fluctuations, accentuations, and the rise and fall of the pitch of each phrase.

What time will you be arriving tomorrow?

I can't believe I won! Wow, I have never won anything before in my life!

This cloudy rainy weather has been so dismal the last two weeks. It really is affecting my mood. When is the sun going to come out again?

The day is young, and the sun is out and shining brilliantly. There are so many possibilities for us to choose from and explore.

Now we can also think about these sentences in a musical phrase context.

Play a musical phrase with not only the same rhythm, accents and pacing that the vowels and consonants convey to you in the previous phrase examples when spoken, but also with the same inflection that is suggested. Now take these into a song adding meter and tempo, and sing or recite them to yourself while playing melodic phrases that match up to the spoken ones. Try to get them to lock into the groove and rhythm of the song.

Nuance Inflection Example

Check out this list of nuances and inflections that you can incorporate into your music:

- the crying effect by playing out of and into bends

- slurs

- staccato note successions

- trills

- oblique intervallic patterns such as John Coltrane used

- pull offs and hammer ons

- using the instrument's extreme ranges

- growls

- slapping

- percussive effects

- touch, air and breath elements

- sustained notes
- dynamics
- double and triple time phrases
- exploiting timbre and tonal variations
- glissandos and slides
- screams
- flutter tonguing
- smears
- muted notes
- volume swells, both up and down
- pick sweeps for plectrum instruments
- flourishes
- textural elements
- shading
- doubling in unison
- distorted effects
- tremolo
- vibrato

The list goes on. Spend some time listening to the players you like for specific nuances and inflections in their own playing and practice using the ones from the list above while improvising on, and playing the melody of different tunes. Don't forget to include these in your compositions as well.

There is a lot here in this first chapter that informs the rhythmic, melodic, harmonic, dynamic, timbric and expressive aspects of our sound and music into a personal auditory fingerprint, so you can just take a little at a time to work with and absorb into your vocabulary. By seeing all of it broken down we can begin to realize what our strengths and weaknesses are and practice them one at a time and eventually in tandem with one another. This is also important to keep in mind with the other areas that come after the sound is put forth including motivic development, phrasing, vocabulary and ear training with all aspects of music. Training the ear is crucial so we can identify with what we are hearing and what the other musicians are playing.

All of this will bring you closer to connecting all areas of sound creation, to what eventually can manifest into a complete expression of yourself in myriad ways through your instrument.

This is a journey for all of us that has no end, just a continued discovery and connection with ourselves through the practice and creation of the art.

Chapter 2 Transcription

Our initiation into learning from others through listening to recordings, osmosis, live performance, and transcription, allows us to develop and garner new vocabulary, rhythms, techniques, articulations, phrasing, time feel, and nuance to name a few. Through this process, we begin to discover what we are attracted to and aligned with regarding players, styles, musical dialects, and so forth. This helps to inform us of the music that resonates the most with us. Also, transcribing solos from other instrumentalists allows us to graft new techniques and ideas that can be applied to our own chosen instrument.

Transcription typically involves these 8 stages:

1. Listening - (for meter, tempo, rhythm, shape, pitch, chord quality and voicing)

2. Singing - (internalizing what you hear)

3. Playing - (optional if doing by ear and singing only)

4. Checking and confirming

5. Notating (use a pencil)

6. Playing - (at tempo or slower if needed, along with, and without the recording. Practice both with and without a metronome).

7. Analyzing and noting points of interest in the solo.

8. Assimilating the material into one's own personal lines, sound and approach.

This last stage of transcription is by far for many people the most elusive and is where the real process begins if we want to utilize what we learn from transcription in a more personal way in our music.

To achieve this it is a good idea to create exercises involving the rhythmic, melodic, harmonic, phrasing, articulation, expressive, and dynamic elements of the material that stand out the most for you. This can help to bridge the gap between the player we transcribe and ourself, by furthering unique traits and pathways of invention to open up in our own playing.

I highly recommend that you play along to recordings as well each day. This helps with internalizing rhythm, time, time feel, phrasing, and a host of other musical skills and abilities that are important to the improvisor's development.

I also have my students write out their own solos on tunes resolving to all the chord and scale degrees for each chord change. Start with chord degrees 1, 3, 5, 7, then the diatonic scale degrees 9, 11, 13, and then include the non-diatonic tensions ♭9, ♯9, ♭13 (or ♯5), and ♯11(or ♭5). Use one degree at a time for each solo at first. Later on you can also write out solos resolving to all the down and up beats of the measure besides the beat that the chord enters on. This is great to practice on static chord progressions with just one or two chords in the form. Resolving to all the beats will also give you a door into asymmetrical phrasing so your lines do not always begin and end on the same beats in a measure. Be able to play, analyze, and internalize all of this over time to discover the specific rhythms, lines, and resolution points that speak to you. Make sure you also use the lines from some of the solos you have transcribed by permutating the melodic contour, rhythm, resolution, and placement along with adding and omitting notes within the lines with your own personal and creative approach and energy.

A very important thing that happens when you play the solo along with the original recording which can be an eye and ear opener for you regarding awareness into your style, is to emulate every aspect of the solo's content as if you were tracing it with an auditory pencil. You may find sometimes to your disappointment that there is something that is not as exacting or is different from the original. So just as when you try to trace a person's signature, (no sweat, I know you're not a forger) we will never be totally spot on. With this you discover that what you think is missing in your playing in reference to the original, is not actually anything missing at all, but rather a kind of epiphanic discovery of the aspects of your own identity that are revealed and emerging. These can show up in your phrasing, little quirks in how you approach a note, rhythm, attack, and even your errors and a host of other areas to look out and listen for.

We must also simply improvise a lot using what we gain from transcription along with what we have already acquired from our experience in a creative way to go even deeper within ourselves towards what we want to hear and how we want to play. A little transcription goes a long way if we dive deeper into it, covering the aforementioned areas and exercises in detail, and coming away with much more than if we were to transcribe a lot of solos and just brush the surface of them.

Lastly, once you have any type of recorded output of yourself, it is important that you analyze your own playing to decipher what is truly yours in respect to all that has been previously mentioned. I will go back to my own recordings sometimes and try to find just one idea from each piece that has meaning for me and include the idea in as many different ways as possible in my playing. Look for attributes and subtleties in not only the main sound dimensions of rhythm, melody, harmony, timbre, texture, and dynamics, but also the way notes are played and phrases are delivered. Again, also explore contour, attack, touch, nuance, intonation, time feel, and groove. Then go deeper!

What is the feeling inside you when playing? Is there a powerful electrical and emotional energy going through you from your connection to the music? For me and many others, the most important aspect of playing and hearing music is the feeling, energy and heart that manifests in you from the music.

In this you will find the true core or furnace of your sound that can be developed with a depth and ability to project outward to anyone, since you are feeling this energy so strongly inside yourself. When I was much younger I referred to this energy as an electric eel that was surging through me. I was not aware at the time that this was the naturally occurring electricity that our biology generates within us, and at that early stage could only describe the feeling that I experienced in this way.

Learning Solos Without Transcription

You can approach transcription in a few different ways. One way if you are new to transcribing will be for you to learn some easier solos, or at least some sections of solos you like by ear first, committing them to memory without writing them out. When you do this, you exercise and develop your brain and musical memory skills in different ways than if you were to actually write down the solo for the purpose of sight-reading at a later date, since the material you learn needs to be repeated enough to be memorized and played.

The best way to achieve this is to keep playing and singing (even if you are not a singer), the solo or passage from the beginning each time you learn and add a new phrase. There are several areas that you can be taking care of at the same time by doing it this way. You will not only memorize the solo, but you will also be able to execute the whole solo through to the end by the time you learn the last phrase since you would have been repeatedly playing the solo all the way through from the beginning up to the point of each new line being added. It is also a good idea at this point to try and bring the solo up to the original tempo if you need to play it slower at first. These tips are also great to keep in mind when you are writing out the solo, since when you have completed the transcription you will still need to be able to play the entire solo at tempo.

Before I was even into jazz, I learned and memorized many solos in other styles of music this way without notating the music I was learning. This was very helpful with improving rhythmic and melodic skills, memorization, and other abilities needed when I actually did begin transcribing jazz solos. The memorization development was particularly invaluable for acquiring the skills needed in memorizing music for the groups I would be involved with in the future, since this aspect of musicianship is a must for professional musicians in many genres.

Learning Solos With Transcription

After you confirm the meter and tempo of the solo you are transcribing, be sure to confirm which beat the first note falls on and if there is a pickup measure present that the solo begins with prior to the start of the solo's form. It can be a good idea if you are new to transcription to sketch out a rhythm map of the solo first. This will allow you to focus on just the rhythm so you can align all the notes correctly with the beats of each measure using just note stems. Count the down beats and up beats of each measure during, and again slowly after each phrase you are listening for to keep track of, and determine the subdivisions, note values, number of notes, and rhythms being played. Once you have confirmed that all the rhythms and phrases are accurate you can then add the pitches and other elements to the solo. You can do this either with music manuscript paper or in a music engraving program if you use one. Here are two examples of how you can notate just the rhythm at first so you can add in the remainder of the solo's content later on.

Transcription Rhythm Examples

Ex. 1

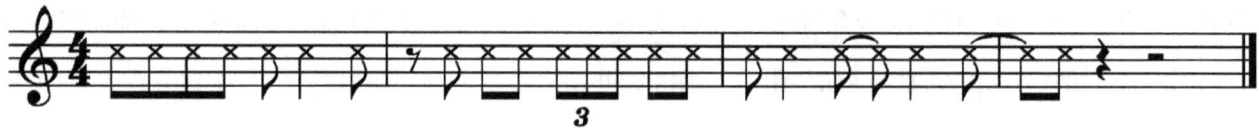

Ex. 2

When you are ready to notate the pitches, you can use the piano or your own instrument to help you learn the solo. Notating the pitches can be challenging for many. A good place to start if you are having trouble discerning any pitches in the phrases being played is to listen for the contour or shape of the passage you are trying to transcribe and notate first.

Along with the contour it is also very helpful to find the first and last notes. Targeting the first and last notes of each phrase as shown in the following pitch example, will help you in discerning the missing notes between each target note, because since these target notes exist as the lower and higher extremities of each phrase they usually will stand out amongst the other notes in between.

Transcription Pitch Example

Some people have used aids to slow down the recording to help facilitate learning the notes, like an older turntable set to 16 rpm, (bringing the notes down twice as slow and one octave below), or other digital devices for slowing the recording down without changing the pitch. Although these tools can be helpful in learning about what you are not hearing and allow for advancing in some ways, I would suggest you always try your best and do this alone with your own ears first and resort to these tools later if you need to for confirming the accuracy of the solo.

The above approach in the pitch example can also be very helpful when learning the various voicings of chords that may be played in the solo. Again, the extremities of the chord, or the lowest and highest notes will stand out more clearly at first and help us to work downward from the highest note, or upward from the lowest note to determine the exact voicing of the chord. You also need to listen to the chord qualities like major, minor, augmented, and diminished triads, and all the four and five note voicings that stem out from these triads. When discerning the voicing, listen for the density of the chord being played. Are the notes very close together as in a closed voice chord, or are they more spread out as with an open voicing. By being aware of these areas we can sharpen our aural abilities, allowing us to determine more information from our hearing and less from trial and error.

Transcribing Without an Instrument

The next way to transcribe is by ear without using an instrument and is a more advanced approach by singing the parts out loud and then notating them. Once you have the first note or notes from the recording confirmed, sing the next series of notes out loud and use relative or absolute pitch to determine the intervals, various linear and vertical type lines, and rhythms between each note or phrase and notate the solo this way. This is excellent for your auditory development and ear training, and will help you to realize the ability to see what you hear for notation. Sight singing a solo or melody already transcribed and realized would be the opposite, hearing and singing what you see.

When you are finished transcribing and are working on executing the solo, you should have a pretty good grasp of singing the entire solo while playing it.

Do your best to try and learn to sing any difficult passages. This will help you connect with, internalize, and express the solo even deeper. I cannot emphasis enough the importance of singing and playing what you hear for the development of your future musicality in every aspect and way. Be sure to also play the solo as best you can along with the recording as well as alone both with and without a metronome.

Solo Analysis

Take the time to note down any points of interest and highlights that stand out to you from the solo. This will be what you take away from the solo that can be infused with the musical traits you already have when you improvise.

Make note of any specific rhythmic, melodic, harmonic, timbric, and textural elements as well as nuance, inflection, ornamentation, dynamics, and other expressive aspects in the solo.

You can transcribe entire solos or just specific lines from solos that have meaning for you, and take them through the eight transcription stages listed. Do this for solos not only on your own instrument but for other instruments as well. Saxophone, trumpet and vocal solos are great for teaching piano and guitar players about phrasing and economy, since the latter instrumentalists can continue breathing while playing, and can learn a lot from the former who must incorporate rest and the breath along with their musical lines.

Chapter 3 Composition

Composition has always been important in regard to developing and personalizing our own sound and style further.

In the beginning, I intentionally tried to write pieces that were in the styles of the music that I was listening to that inspired me. This was growing all the time as I came across new players and styles through the ever-expanding musical tree. I think of these pieces and the years I spent writing them (about 10 years) as an apprenticeship in small group writing.

It was a blast to try and write small group pieces in the progressive styles of Lee Morgan, Joe Henderson or Woody Shaw, as well as more modal writing, tunes with bi-tonal chords, ostinato patterns, abstract unison melodies, chamber music harmonies, and more open forms with and without meter or chord changes inspired by Ornette Coleman, Don Cherry, and the freer approaches coming from the various northern European transcultural roots which also included my own.

The tunes I felt had something to offer were a catalyst for me to start performing with my own groups, and continue to study much more about the many musical devices and elements utilized by composers and arrangers to write stronger and more personal music.

I did come to realize in part the truth of the saying that "you only have ten songs in you". I would start to see new pieces emerge that were a direct relation to an earlier piece, but still unique in their own right. Like siblings in a family who look alike but also retain their own personality and identity, or the Son of Godzilla to Godzilla.

Through this so-called compositional apprenticeship I had unearthed some meaningful personal musical traits for myself in my writing, which were then, and still are in part, reflected back into my playing over time. It is an ongoing process. You have to write a lot, and be very particular about what you are willing to accept and rule out for yourself in the process.

Here are four composition exercises you can check out.

Exercise 1: Beginning the History of Your Composition

Begin or complete a composition with the following chord, Cmaj9. You can voice it any way you want using the various open and closed voiced forms, or even with just a four note voicing leaving out the fifth.

Try to at least have around a four bar cadence or phrase completed, or a completed piece if that happens, but don't force things along. Try to listen to what you hear in your mind's ear as the next event after you play the first chord and before you play anything else. This could be in the form of a second chord, a melody, or another event you add. The important thing to keep in mind here is the history and direction of the piece can begin just from the new event being added to the starting chord. Here are some devices and ideas to use:

1. You can use harmony throughout your process to help support the gravity and frame of the melody as you develop your cadences.

2. Try to develop a strong melody from your first motif. This will influence and allow you to hear the next harmonic event resulting in less trial and error and preventing the piece from sounding forced.

3. There are no limits to our imagination. Use these compositional devices for inspiration and development.

- Ostinato melodies and bass lines

- Counterpoint, the art of intervals, like using only a bass line with the melody line, where the two lines suggest and outline the harmony. Use oblique, similar, parallel, compound melody, and contrary motion to create melodic and harmonic foundations for ideas.

- Pedal points
- Bitonal or polychords
- Constant structure
- Asymmetrical time signatures
- Rhythmic figures
- Unison melodies
- Broken chords (arpeggio) or melted chords
- Block chords
- Inversions
- Chord or interval cycles (cycle 3, cycle 4, Coltrane cycles and rhythm changes, and various blues structures)
- Closed voicings
- Interval clusters (tighter than closed voicings)
- Open voicings (Drop 2, Drop 3, Drop 2 & 4 or Drop 2 & 3)
- Harmonized scales to develop progressions, key centers, and transposition.
- Just melody all by itself can be a beautiful thing too.
- Triads

4. Of course with the above you can include many styles to compose with such as ballad, waltz, swing, bossa nova, samba, or influences drawn from baião, calypso, Afro Cuban, free/rubato, blues, merengue, numerous African dialects, Caribbean, impressionism (think Ravel or Debussy), African 12/8, Indian konnakol, Euro folk influences etc.

Exercise 1. Composition Examples

Ex1. Inversions
Ballad

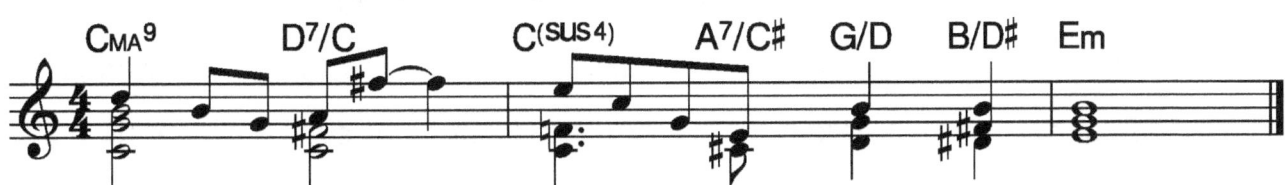

Ex 2. Pedal Point
Ballad

Ex 3. Bi - Tonal Chords
Ballad

Ex 4. Same Chord/ Parallel Motion
Even 8ths

Ex 5. Bass Ostinato/Assymetrical Time Signatures
Even 8ths

© 2014 Jim Robitaille Music

Exercise 2: Composing with Modes

I have done this exercise with many students over the years as it helps to develop both personalized compositional and improvisational skills. You can write it out if you want, but you will at least need a recorder to create what you will improvise to, or even better at times, have another person to perform these with. Try to sense what mood the mode conveys to you. Some are major or minor in quality, so this can help you along your way.

Our purpose with this exercise is twofold. One is to develop and explore the two to eight measure ideas we compose by using these modes through improvisation, allowing possible areas of the composition to unfold with a creative realtime approach. The other purpose is to have a vehicle to further our improvising in a more personal realm with our own composed ideas without the need to have an entire piece completed.

1. Start by taking each mode of the diatonic scale one at a time and improvise a short two to four or eight bar pattern or section on each mode. Be creative, and make good use of the musical devices we have at our disposal from exercise 1.

2. Once you have something, record it for at least five minutes, or loop it.

3. Now you can improvise on it anytime in the future. You can also play these with different musicians. Record what you improvise on it with and then listen for the musical ideas and phrases that you like and develop those further for new vocabulary or sketches for compositions. For example, if you play a rhythm pattern that you like in one section, bring that into all the other modes and sections you created and play it with those as well. This will ingrain the idea even further by letting you hear it with the other modes and patterns, which is a necessary skill to develop that is used all the time in composition and improvisation. Stay open to the possibility that these sections can be developed into full-fledged compositions too. I have had several students do this as a result of working with this exercise. It is also very important to transpose them to all keys.

Major Scale Modes

1. Ionian (Diatonic, major)

2. Dorian (Minor b3, b7)

3. Phrygian (Almost a Spanish minor, b2, b3, b6, b7)

4. Lydian (#4)

5. Mixolydian (b7)

6. Aeolian (Natural minor, b3, b6, b7)

7. Locrian (The darkest of them all. b2, b3, b5, b6, b7)

You can do this for any of the other common scales and their modes as well like harmonic minor, melodic minor, harmonic major, and even symmetrical diminished scales can be interesting.

Exercise 2. Composition Examples

© 2014 Jim Robitaille Music

Exercise 3: Composing With One Chord Quality and Motif

Write a tune with only one chord quality at a time and develop a melody with a single motif. Again, it can be just a cadence to start, but sometimes a tune just writes itself and we are left wondering where it all came from.

Since we are working within the limitation of having the same chord quality for each new chord, we can change key as much as we want. With our intention, the chords can seemingly take on the energy and various functions that exist with the usual chord qualities we are accustomed to, such as, (the common II V I cadence). II is typically minor and is leading, V7 is dominant seventh and is restless and creates ambiguity, and I is major or minor and resolves and brings it all home. This can also help us to develop a more heighten aural sense and awareness for each chord quality which will be useful when composing with many chords types together as is more often the case.

Chord Types to use.

<u>All Triads</u>

Major, Minor, Diminished, Augmented

<u>All Major Types</u>.

Maj6, Maj7, Maj9, Maj6/9, Maj6/7, Maj7(♯5), Maj7(♯11), Maj9(♯11)

<u>All Minor Types</u>

min6, min♭6, min7, min(Ma7), min9, min6/9, min7♭5, min11

All Dominant Seventh Types

7th, sus4, 9th, 13th, 7(♭9), 7(♯9), 7(♭13), 7(♯11), or any combination of these tensions as well.

All Diminished Types

Half Diminished, Dim7, Dim(Ma7)

Did I miss any? You get the idea.

Don't forget about using the inversions of these chords as well.

Creating a melody from a single motif is one of the oldest and most common and useful approaches to melodic development and embellishment in composition and improvisation. From Early music to modern day pop songs and improvised solos, there are endless examples throughout musical history to learn from with motivic development.

There are a few jazz pieces floating about that have the same quality of chords and motifs mostly throughout, if not all the way through. Joe Henderson's "Inner Urge", "Patterns" by Oliver Nelson, "Time Remembered" by Bill Evans, and "The Real Guitarist in the House" by Steve Kuhn. I have a few pieces that come to mind. Here is a ballad called "Back To Bayeux".

Chapter 3 Composition 53

Composition Example 3: Back To Bayeux

© 2010 Jim Robitaille Music

Exercise 4: Composing using a Jazz Contrafact

    A contrafact is a very common practice in jazz music where you write an original melody based on the chord progression to another tune. Make use of all the previously mentioned musical devices. Use your imagination, and listen closely for what the song suggests to you. There are many examples of this in jazz such as "Donna Lee" composed by Charlie Parker, which is based on the song "Back Home Again in Indiana". The numerous songs and harmonic variations of George Gershwin's "I Got Rhythm" can be found in such classic jazz compositions as Sonny Rollins' "Oleo" and Charlie Parker's "Anthropology". John Coltrane's "Fifth House" is based on the Cole Porter composition "What is This Thing Called Love" and Thelonious Monk's "Evidence", draws on the chords to the standard Just You, Just Me.

    Here is one based on the chord changes to another standard tune.

Lost and Found by Jim Robitaille

    This song has an angular melody that is based loosely on the chord changes to the song "If I Should Lose You" by Ralph Rainger and Leo Robin, and is played in unison by the whole group. The only chord on the melody or head is at the very end of the in and out head. For this arrangement, the original standard tune's chord changes are used for the solos only.

Chapter 3   Composition   55

Composition Example 4: Lost And Found

Chapter 4 Arranging

Bringing your individual ideas and approaches from your original compositions into your arrangements of the music of other composers can breathe new life into someone else's music, truly making it your own.

The song "Yesterdays" by Jerome Kern, is an example of an arrangement I did where some of the musical devices present in my compositions over the years have found their way into various arrangements of standard tunes.

*Yesterdays - Jerome Kern

This is a multi-metered restructuring of the Jerome Kern tune "Yesterdays", born out of the alternating 6/4 and 7/4 vamp that takes place in the intro and first few bars of the tune.

The vamp locks into a specific groove by the rhythmic pattern. The hybrid descending chord pattern was suggested by, and harmonizes with, the ascending melody in measure five. The guitar harmony line moves in contrary motion to the melody.

The result of the multiple meters is that they support the basic inner pulse suggested by the melody and lyrics, therefore sounding completely natural in the context of this type of arrangement.

The other element that I heard and very much wanted was the silence from the break that happens at the end of the melody before the solos on the in and out head. I actually added a melody note and tension here to set this up. I had to, the arrangement was screaming for it. Again, this idea is taken from another art form. Cinema!

Think scene transitions in film here. I love some of the startling atmospheres that have been created by master film directors like Fellini, Kubrick or Kurasawa, where a dramatic result is felt when a scene peaks and ends, and is then followed by the screen going to black for a few seconds, only to segue into the next scene.

The solo section alternates between four measures of 7/4 and four measures of 4/4. The results of the devices used in this arrangement are very much like some of the original music I like to write, and sits alongside it just fine as if it was an original tune.

Arranging allows us to bring our own ears and ideas into the music of other composers. Here we can reharmonize, rearrange, restructure, change time signatures, add intros, interludes, outros and so forth, to bring our musical approach and vision to other music that resonates with us.

Visit www.jimrobitaille.com/store to purchase the optional score and MP3 audio files for "Yesterdays", and the MP3 audio files for the four original composition, and other art form examples in Sound Origins.

Chapter 5 Improvisation

When I think back on the origins of how I started playing music and the guitar, I improvised for many hours with the music I was exposed to growing up. I did not even stop to think about what an improviser was back then. I would play along to the radio, records, alone, or with other guitarists, since I did not know any bassists or drummers to hook up with yet. Improvising amused me, the process taught me a lot, and I really loved experiencing the creative flow, chance taking, and exploration that took place within it. Like many guitarists at that time, I was completely self-taught, not taking any formal lessons until about three or four years after I began.

This time period enabled me to develop a pretty alert ear, imagination, awareness of trying to get a good sound from the hands and the instrument, some technique, rhythm, licks, fluency, and an overall good rhythmic feel for the different types of rock and blues music I was hearing and playing. This is no different than the way we absorb our parents' language by ear before we learn to read and write it later on. I hardly knew any tunes at all at the time, so when someone asked me to play something, I would usually just improvise for them. I had no idea about jazz music or anything like that until later.

While playing many styles of music over the years, it came as no surprise to me that this totally spontaneous and intuitive approach to playing that I took during my youth (especially the skills developed by playing along to recordings) prepared and informed me for the music that I eventually became so drawn to and involved with professionally.

In music or any endeavor, when you are doing something spontaneous and in the now, all your facilities are working in sync on an intuitive level that connects you very deeply with responding to whatever is taking place at that moment. The guided mind and trusted instincts are working as one.

Did you ever think about who the first improviser was in music? We have the great composers from centuries past like Johann Sebastian Bach and Wolfgang Amadeus Mozart who were master improvisers or spontaneous composers of the Baroque and Classical eras. In jazz music, maybe it was some creative soul quite possibly even before Joe King Oliver, Louis Armstrong or Jelly Roll Morton. How did it go down? Did they make a mistake and respond in the moment to survive and keep the music from deflating on the spot? Or was the improvisation intentional, or possibly out of boredom, because they had played the same piece the same way so many times before?

If we think about these possibilities, we can come to learn and understand more about our natural response and reason for hearing and playing the way we do. How do we react to the music or our playing when we play something? If we played it, then we must have intended it, right? Can we even actually play something we did not intend? Do we make it a mistake by living in the past moment, or react to it in a more positive developmental way that is in the present time? Do we take chances and try to respond from the feeling within us, or if we become a little dispassionate, do we try to find new inspiration in the same music we often find ourselves playing, reinventing it, and ourselves to some degree?

With improvisation, we are always in and responding to the *now*. That's in life too! We are all improvisors 24/7, even in our dreams. Nobody hands you a script each day to follow (unless you're an actor or actress). We are masters at reacting and adapting and being flexible and ready to go with the flow, because there is no past or future when you are in the moment, just moving towards the next moment which will always be the next now. By developing awareness in this way we can drop into the moments more easily and consistently without the effort of trying at all when we begin playing music.

There are many great creative concepts, techniques, devices, musical elements, materials, ear training for developing relative and absolute pitch skills (a must since the source of the music comes through and from you, and not from the instrument), and much more that are readily available to us in our musical education. These will help further anyone's vocabulary when learning and practicing the art of improvisation. However, none of these will be completely effective musically if we do not truly relate to and take part in the actual inner process of what the true nature of improvising really is and means, which is simply being present with, and responding in, the moment.

Here are a few other things to keep in mind that can be helpful as well when studying, playing and improvising:

- Become adept at the function of your solo and supportive roles.
- Develop with attention to detail, a lot of rhythmic, melodic, harmonic, expressive, and dynamic vocabulary to communicate with.
- Don't forget about all the variants pertaining to your instrument's timbre.
- Be aware of the contour and shape of your solos.
- Know the emotion and feeling you are trying to convey, and how that relates to the music at hand. Even humor has its place at times in music.
- Hearing what you want to play, and the ability to play it (playing what you hear) are two different things.
- Take chances. Perfection is an illusion. Is there a perfect tree in the forest? Getting to the rare moments that can only be achieved in an improvisational time space is worth the price of living with what we may call imperfection.
- Solo construction. Approaching various ways to construct the beginning, middle and end of your solos.
- Learn as much as you can about motivic development. Remember what was mentioned

earlier about our spoken language and expressing coherent ideas.

- Developing consistency even on your off nights is a big part of being a pro.

- Get in there and play with the rhythm section, both as a soloist and accompanist. Know where your beat placement and time feel need to be at any moment in relation to the rhythm section.

- Be supportive, lead, follow, stir it up, let it out and hold it back when needed, and be ready to turn on a dime with the band.

- Develop a good editing mind. Very helpful for both live performance and recording sessions.

- Try to perform live with the consistent mindset you would want for yourself in the studio. Likewise, try to perform in the studio and go for it with the energy you have in live performance.

- Learn as much as you can about the functions of the instruments and instrumentalists you perform with. This can help you to realize what your function is or is not at any given time in the music.

- Keep working on your sound to bring to fruition what you hear in your mind's ear. The more connected and developed this is for you, the more you will like what you hear and will play from the heart.

- You can only fill your own shoes, and no one will even know they exist, including you, until you step into them.

- It can be very beneficial for you to spend some time learning to play more open and freer forms of music. When you improvise on a song you know very well from a form, you are bringing a *freedom* of expression to that song. You can approach it freely and in a loose way because of your familiarity with its framework. On the other hand when you play music starting with no form, you enter into a space where you may start with nothing at all, with complete freedom, and form needs to be developed and allowed to unfold within the musical events that take place resulting in a type of spontaneous composition. Jazz musicians need both sides of the coin here. Form can teach us about freedom, and freedom teaches us about developing and improving our abilities with form. It is curious to note that the two main styles of jazz to inherently have collective improvisation are New Orleans traditional dixieland and ragtime jazz, and the free, avant garde or open form jazz of the 1960's.

- Let influences be just what they are, a natural occurring thread in the larger fabric of your musical self.

- Chromaticism has existed in all forms of music including popular, jazz, opera, and serialism and twelve-tone technique since the latter half of the 19th century. It offers a pitch palette of expression for composers and improvisors to further expand their ideas and playing. A must to study!

- Transcribe solos or lines of your favorite players to expand your vocabulary.

- Remember whatever a composer learns is what an improviser can learn too, but in real time.

- Remember again, what an improviser learns is what a composer can learn in slowed down time.

In closing this chapter, it is important to be familiar with the many types of improvisors that exist. Some of us play solely by ear, with little or no knowledge of standard music nomenclature, but with an internal self taught intelligence that allows for maneuvering all the musical elements that make up a piece of music when we improvise. I feel this internal ability is a must for all improvisors, and ultimately can only be developed with the ears and our musical instincts and experience. Some others have this ability to varying degrees, and also read music and garner a working knowledge of music theory, harmony, counterpoint, arranging, orchestration, and composition along the way. Some musicians enter into the improvisational world with classical music backgrounds. This is common for many types of instrumentalists, who quite often bring with them an impressive technique on their respective instruments. Some musicians enter into the improvisational world with a good technique on their instrument and strong sight reading abilities, but with little experience and knowledge of improvisation. With a world of improvisational and compositional resources and approaches available to us now, we all can pursue furthering our knowledge and skills with this art form.

Today it is expected that improvisors be complete musicians and have a working knowledge of their instrument, technique, music theory, functional harmony, twentieth century harmony, jazz harmony, improvisational concepts and approaches, a lot of vocabulary, and a good ear to understand what they are hearing and to be able to express and play what they hear in response.

With this awareness, we can develop the areas needed to improve and fulfill our musicianship in a way that allows for us to more easily drop in and spontaneously connect with each moment in the music.

Chapter 6 The Art of Listening

When we focus on listening closely to the other musicians we are playing with we can become more aware of what's taking place within the music at hand as well as listening to ourselves in regards to what we play, how we sound, and how we respond to it. The reverse is true as well in many cases. When we begin playing music with others, we have not yet developed the skills to be able to spread out our ears and listen outside of ourselves attentively to the other players, or even to ourselves for that matter.

Something I recommend to students is to play in a duo a lot in the beginning to start and set this process in motion. (It is also often easier to find one other player, rather than three or four at a time, and a lot of other things can also be learned in the process of playing in a duo, such as developing good time, for instance.) By becoming more adept at listening to just one other person besides ourselves, we can develop the awareness, focus, and ability that is needed to listen further into the music when we find ourselves in larger groups with three or more musicians down the line. So if you are a student in school, coerce that flute player or pianist into the practice room with you and play one another's music. You may generate new friendships and discover future professional connections in the process, and a lot can be learned in the discussions you have in between the music being played.

When you listen to recordings, choose several that have varied instrumentation from solo all the way up to large ensembles and practice this listening ability until you start to notice a shift in your scope and awareness with the various parts you are hearing. Here is another thing to check out.

The next time you are in a conversation with a group of three or more people, imagine likening it to being in that size musical group. Notice how the various participants, listen, speak, interact, interject, lay out, jump in, or how they may interrupt, not listen, and only say what they have to say without regard to what others say. Also notice how the conversation evolves. Does it stay on one topic, resolving, or does it segue into other areas?

Performing improvised music is conversational. Listening is essential, and like a conversation in our spoken language, the result will not happen to any desirable degree without it.

So if we listen closer to who we are performing with, we can hear and appreciate what is being played by the other musicians. This will allow us to become further immersed in what is actually taking place in the music at any given moment. Listening will also help us to follow and guide the content of the music we play by being more in tune with our own musical output. In turn this can also teach us to point our ears within ourselves and grasp listening closer in relation to what we're hearing and processing, and how we respond and interact with the music and the other musicians.

Chapter 7 Other Art Forms

Visual Arts

It can be a good idea to get away from music to gain perspective with it sometimes. You develop your art as you live it. Everything in life has an effect on us to some extent, and therefore will inevitably influence our art in some way.

The visual arts, particularly painting, was one of my first influences outside of music. Though I am not a painter myself, there are a few musicians that are, or were, like Miles Davis, Joni Mitchell, Tony Bennett, Bob Dylan, Ron Wood, and John Lennon to name a few. The famous conductor Leopold Stokowski, who also appeared in the Disney film "Fantasia", was quoted saying, "A painter paints his pictures on canvas, but musicians paint their pictures on silence."

Some of my favorite painters and or sculptors whose works I have been fortunate enough to see are: Vincent Van Gogh, Camille Pissarro, Pablo Picasso, Claude Monet, Paul Cézanne, Edgar Degas, Salvador Dali, Pierre Auguste Renoir, Wassily Kandinsky, Francisco Goya, Joan Miro, Auguste Rodin, Georges Seurat, Jackson Pollock, Andy Warhol, Rembrandt Van Rijn, Paul Signac and many others. Check out Impressionism, Fauvism, Surrealism, Abstract Expressionism, Cubism or still life if that is your thing.

Over the years I have loved the diversion of using paintings as vehicles to try and compose music from, but nothing ever resulted in any completed works for years really. I knew for myself that the many similarities existing between the two art forms could yield new ideas and music that I wanted to explore. I eventually had a few pieces come together fortunately.

I composed a work while looking at a painting by Joan Miro. I simply called the piece "Miro" along with the subtitle (composition in 3/4 for seven modes and six pedal points). Another tune I wrote entitled "Figures", was inspired by the positive and negative space found in figure drawing.

Chapter 7 Other Art Forms   67

Visual Arts Example: Figures

Figures

Jim Robitaille

Med Swing

1st time w/ bass & drums only
Rhythm section plays off the head for solos

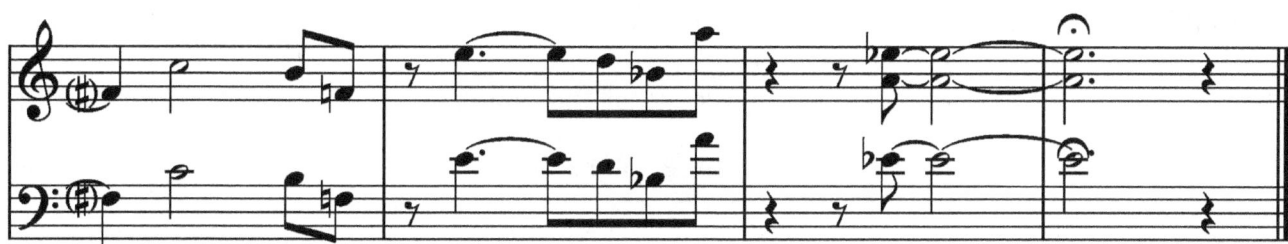

Fine

© Jim Robitaille Music 1998

There are so many parallels within each art form. For example, take the elements that make up a work of art, and compare them to both music and painting, or any other art forms you may desire. All art disciplines contain form, structure, light or sound vibration, color, shading and hue, dimension, line, shape, dynamics, negative and positive space, and some more I could mention. I am sure you can think of some others.

I encourage you to check out the many great art museums and galleries worldwide in your travels. The Guggenheim in New York (designed by the great *architectural* master Frank Lloyd Wright, there's another art form) and the Metropolitan Museum of Art are two examples.

One time on my way back from a tour I went to the Salvador Dali museum in St. Petersburg, Florida. One couple owns this museum's entire art collection, and they have some of his most important works, including some paintings of landscapes when he was very young prior to his surrealist period. One earlier painting that he reproduced again a few years later in the surreal style was in comparison to the original, a very revealing glimpse into his beginnings as a modernist. The museum houses the largest collection of Dali paintings in the world.

If you have not taken the opportunity already, I am certain you won't walk away the same person if you make the time to bring this art discipline into your life and experience the many positive influences it can have on your music.

Poetry

There is a lot that can be deciphered and grafted into music from poetry pertaining to the pacing and phrasing that are so important to this art form.

A very dear friend introduced me to the works of the great Austrian German poet Rainer Maria Rilke. There was a poem that moved me entitled "To Music". He wrote several variations on this theme, but there was a specific one that stirred me enough to have the record label obtain the license to include it on the panel of my recording by the same name coincidentally. This guy sure knew how to phrase!

Literature

I have been very inspired by the late science journal and essay writer, visionary, inventor, and science fiction novelist Arthur C. Clarke. He was a strong influence on several fronts. The great director Stanley Kubrick (Remember the inspiration that came from film mentioned earlier in the arranging chapter), made Clarke's book 2001: A Space Odyssey, into the famous film of the same title. I don't typically read much science fiction at all, but Arthur C. Clarke wrote science articles, and in these and his many well known books he made predictions about space travel that came to be true in very important areas such as the early Apollo missions. His published essays on the concepts that led to the communication satellite inspired and helped along the technology years before it ever came into fruition.

His books are what he called "Science Fact", instead of Science Fantasy or Science Fiction. Everything he wrote was backed up with science facts, even though they seemed either unbelievable at the time, or had not yet come to pass. For instance in his 1978 novel "Fountains of Paradise" there is a copy of the congressional patent of a proven anti-gravity belt from the 1930's. (I guess they never released that one to the public.) The use of this technology, again inspired by Clarke's novel, has led NASA scientists to publishing statements that it is possible for them to create an actual escalator to space stations which was the premise of Clarke's novel.

After reading his novel "Rendezvous With Rama" I was very inspired to compose a piece that captured the surreal visual atmosphere that the story conveyed throughout.

I remember the first half of the tune coming together pretty quickly, but the second half I had to keep at for about two years to complete. Composing seems a lot like guiding the music trying to come through that is waiting for you to connect with it to bring it into fruition. Whatever amount of time and effort it takes I feel is a given and always worth while for the truth of the work to emerge.

You never know when and how inspiration will enter into your life, so it is a good idea to keep your eyes, ears, heart and mind open to all the possibilities that may be revealed to you.

Literature Example: Arthur C.

Nature

I would say nature is an art form. I also feel that it is the greatest of all art forms by the greatest of all artists, whoever or whatever that may be for us.

We learn music from others through teachings, literature, recordings and live performances. These are all coming from people like ourselves who are born both from, and out of nature. We are a small part of nature, but like everything else in it, a very significant part. When we are in our natural surroundings, something speaks very deeply within us. Just notice how you feel when you are by the ocean, in the mountains, or in the forest. Witness how all people are drawn to it, and have the same affinity for these places as we do. It makes sense because we are also a part of what we are seeing and at one with it when witnessing the natural world. It can affect some people even on a deeper level especially if they hardly ever get out of the city or the house. This is a powerful way to clear the clutter and internal dialogue of the mind and get in tune with the self. It really can create a void in us if we don't have this contact with nature in our lives in many ways, since this is where we come from, and what we are made up of, and is an important connection that grounds us.

You can see the deterioration in the modern world where many are losing touch with and depriving themselves of their very own nature. Animals know this firsthand and have been showing us the way for thousands of years. We can definitely learn a lot from them about our own nature as well.

Look at all the great music from composers inspired by the natural world. Maurice Ravel, Claude Debussy, Aaron Copland, Joaquín Rodrigo, Ralph Towner, Antônio Carlos Jobim, Central African Pygmy music, Egberto Gismonti, diaphonic Bulgarian vocal music, and all the great folk and ethnic music inspired by so many indigenous places on the planet. This can be a great basis of inspiration and growth for all of us that puts us back in touch with our source.

Chapter 8 Travel and Other Cultures

Traveling to other countries can have a positive effect on you with not only seeing different cultures and how the people live, but also with obtaining a clearer perspective on your own homeland and life from outside your country. The music, art, food, and lifestyle of others can be a very positive influence on us in many respects.

Duke Ellington embraced many of the cultural influences that were garnered from his travels and experiences in his many suites. Check out "The Far East Suite" or "The Peer Gynt Suite", his version of the "Nutcracker Suite", the "Queen's Suite", the "Latin American Suite" and the "New Orleans Suite". I like to go back to these from time to time. I feel his music truly transcends genre and time.

The jazz fusion group "Weather Report" had a tremendous effect on that genre of music, creating some of the most incredible musical innovations of that time period. Their music was influenced by the global musical cultures of the Caribbean, Africa, Egypt, the United States, Brazil, and Asia.

Meeting the people from other cultures can be invaluable for expanding your character and musical growth. When I first started to perform with my own groups, I was very interested in performing with musicians from many different countries. One reason for this was to hear how they would fit with my music, but also to learn from them, since a lot of the music I had been listening to for many years was recorded abroad and featured many international musicians and new hybrids of jazz. I also felt the inner pull or draw of my own European roots and observed how they were a significant part of what was naturally emerging in my own music. Fortunately I was living in the Northeastern part of the U.S. where many excellent international musicians gravitated to from their respective countries.

Over the years I have been fortunate to perform and record with many musicians and teach students from different regions of Africa, Canada, Brazil, Argentina, Colombia, Central America, Peru, England, Ireland, Scotland, Sweden, Denmark, Norway, Holland, Belgium, United States, Germany, France, Italy, Switzerland, Poland, Russia, Portugal, Hungary, Bulgaria, Cuba, Puerto Rico, Mexico, the West Indies, Israel, Armenia, Lebanon, Pakistan, Cape Verde Islands, India, Australia, Thailand, Japan, Korea, and China.

Music is a common and very powerful language shared among all cultures on earth. Because of this, it brings forth rich exchanges among people with its positive universal communication, celebration, garnered awareness of our shared existence on the planet, and a greater appreciation of the diversity we all can take part in and learn from.

There is no substitute for traveling and what can be gained, and now that the world is smaller in these respects, we can find these cultural riches and exchanges right in our own community.

Chapter 9 Internal Health. Energy, Essence and Spirit

Since performing on an instrument, using your voice, and composing music involves the physical body, it is a good idea to understand what comes before this and governs the body. Remember earlier when I spoke about the importance of going deeper within ourselves to discover more, and not just what appears outside of us. This book is actually something that is outside of you, but is creating awareness for you to go within.

As musicians we can sometimes be led into more taxing life styles aside from our regular daily life such as working late nights, teaching, traveling long distances, sleeping less if you also work a day gig, carting gear, setting aside time for practicing and the occasional aberrated club owner or mobster.

This lifestyle can take its toll. If you want to do this for a long time it will be wise to safeguard your health along the way.

There is a very important energy practice in the Chinese internal martial arts called qigong (pronounced chee-kung), which helps guard the "Three Treasures". The Three Treasures are Jing, Qi and Shen, translated as Essence, Vitality or Energy, and Spirit.

These comprise the three levels of existence for all living beings: physical, energetic, and mental.

Jing or Essence of Life.

The three forms of Jing are:

- Blood essence
- Hormone essence
- Lymph essence and joint and connective tissue lubricants in the body.

These are our precious bodily fluids. If protected they will positively influence the other energies so we can cultivate health, longevity and spirit throughout our life greatly reducing or eliminating premature degenerative disease.

Qi or Chi. Energy of Life, Breath, Air.

Qi is our silent formless energy that governs bodily movement including the lungs, blood and organ systems, and permeates everywhere and everything. All life forms are animated by qi. This is completely influenced by the jing or essence mentioned above.

Shen. The Spirit of Life.

This encompasses all our mental faculties including rational thought, intuition, spirit, attention, will and ego. Daoism embraces all of these energy systems in union, unlike western dualism which typically separates the spirit from the body.

Qigong practice, if done correctly with mindfulness, will create balance throughout the body's organ and energy systems like the triple burner and the endocrine system.

These areas that govern and produce hormones are at the core and source of our health and have been less recognized in allopathic medicine. Qigong will also help develop your breathing habits by bringing the breath back to its origins by breathing from the diaphragm as we did when we were born, instead of shallow chest breathing.

Occasionally I also practice something called the "Six Syllable Secret". These are healing sounds that are typically done in conjunction with certain qigong movements.

Of course for our purpose here in this book, I am just mentioning some of these practices for consideration. If you are interested in learning more about qigong, there are many books, schools and master teachers that will inform you in this, as well as other internal martial arts and natural laws like tai chi chuan, ying yang theory, macrobiotic cooking and counseling,

Chapter 9 Internal Health, Energy, Essence and Spirit

natural food practices, five elemental activities, Zen, Daoism, and yoga. We know how the many forms of physical exercise, stretching and whole natural foods can positively influence the body and mind in our lives. We can look at these internal arts in very much the same way we care for our physical body.

We are just trying to get to know our authentic selves better. By embracing all aspects of our being we can come closer to learning more about who we are in a more conscious sense, and less so in the man-made world that consumes most individuals.

So what does any of this have to do with developing your musical identity? Everything, I feel, at least from what I have come to learn and am still learning for myself in these areas. Music comes through you and from you. The more in tune and connected we are with the governing energies of what actually keeps us alive in body, mind and spirit, the more life force and health of body/essence, energy/breath and mind/spirit we will live through and emit outward in everything we do, including music. Chi is energy, and music gives forth energy and returns it.

Chapter 10 The Instrument & Equipment - The Machine

With everything involved in learning, assimilating and personalizing our music, we always need to come back to the mechanisms that deliver the actual sound into the music.

The instrument or voice that we speak through is very personal for each one of us. To learn about it is an ever evolving quest. Obtaining the appropriate instrument and equipment that supports our needs as our music evolves is an important part of the whole process.

Singers are fortunate in that they have their instrument with them all the time. However vocalists need to take care regarding vulnerabilities to throat viruses and anything that may lower the immune system, causing them to have to cancel performances. This goes for all of us, of course. This is another place where our internal health can be a good ally for us.

Instrumentalists have a lifetime of searching and reaching plateaus in their quest for the elusive holy grail of sound. Check out this list of necessities, niceties, and accoutrements that all musicians have to acquire and keep up with throughout their musical lifetime.

The Fun Stuff List:

Instruments (very personal for each person, with many materials, choices, brands, luthiers, and features to consider, especially if you have one custom-made or design and make it yourself), mouthpieces, reeds (double reed players have to make their own), mutes, strings, bows, rosin, picks, footstools, pickups, valve oil, slides, bridges, nail files, skins and heads, drums, percussion and mallet instruments (deserves their own list), cymbals, sticks, mallets, amplifiers, electronic pianos, synthesizers, PA systems, tuners, tuning keys, frets, nuts, power tubes, preamp tubes, sheet music, fake books, music stands, instrument stands, fingerboards,

Chapter 10 The Instrument & Equipment – The Machine

microphones, cables, hand trucks, electronic expanders and effects, straps, speakers, pads, stools, cases, covers and bags, and so forth ad infinitum.

Of course it can be a real joy to obtain an instrument or something else that allows us to get closer to the sound that we hear in our heads.

Sometimes issues with our instruments or an inferior acoustical environment can be a distraction even for experienced musicians, so it is best to just obtain what you need at any given time, and try to keep the focus on your connection to the music, the people you perform with, and the audience you play for.

Chapter 11 Overview and Summary

Let's briefly outline and summarize what has been covered here in the book, so we can have a big picture of the many areas that can go into developing and furthering the origins of your sound and style in music.

Intent

Obviously we have our intention to begin with in what we want to say. This encompasses the many ways we approach the first note or idea. Bringing what we have learned from our spoken languages into a musical idiom will help us to be more conscious of the content with what we are trying to say in the music as well.

Micro Steps to Sound Creation

When we begin to produce a sound, we have the whole spectrum of micro steps in the creation of the sound that need to be addressed in reference to sound reproduction such as touch, attack, tone, articulation, and dynamics. From there we have a whole other world of musical expression in ornamentation, phrasing, expression and nuance that will breathe life into the sound and ideas we want to express.

Transcription

With transcription, we have the chance to learn from the past and present, and stand on the shoulders of others who came before us. Much is to be learned here regarding sound, vocabulary, rhythm, time, motivic development, harmony, assimilation, emulation, analysis, execution, and all the ways these aspects of the language can be used and incorporated into our music.

Composition

In composition we can study the numerous innovations and styles of music, and emulate and transcend them in our own writing. The many musical elements and devices available to composers are perfect springboards to expand the ways in how we can approach a composition. In time, we can see how these tools will help to develop and realize the conception of our writing style.

Arranging

When we arrange music by others, we have a whole palette to draw from in regards to reharmonizing, restructuring, rearranging, expansion, contraction, and even at times changing the melody to some degree if it pulls you there. Arranging is a powerful tool to develop your own compositional approaches and conception, allowing for your arrangements to stand right alongside your own compositions.

Improvisation

If you are an improvisor, then you have a great way to get in touch with your innermost self and expression. All the elements of the language along with ear training and the ways to use them, are at your disposal. All of our being is taking part in the act of improvising. This pertains to both the completely self taught player, and the player who also knows the entire musical nomenclature.

Try to always be creative, use your imagination, and play from the heart, and remember what was said earlier about everything that a composer learns is what an improvisor can utilize too, and vice versa.

The Art of Listening

When developing listening skills in music, it can be effective to spend time playing and listening to just one other person besides yourself in the beginning, as in a duo. With this in time, you can become more adept and relaxed with your facility to listen to several musicians at once when performing in larger groups. We also spoke about how conversation in our spoken language can alert us to the art of listening in regards to bettering our own skills in this area. In music, especially improvised, it is just as crucial that we use this ability to bring a conversational approach to our music, allowing us to respond, interact, and actually hear what is being played by everyone involved, including ourselves.

Other Art Forms

All the art forms are right before us much of the time. As we live and absorb culture and life, they can inform and inspire our personal avenues in how they appear in our own work. Stay open to their stimuli whenever you go to a gallery, museum, theater, concert, when you read a book, go somewhere in the natural world, have a conversation, or are hanging out with your cat, dog, or the friendly neighborhood boa constrictor. Art and form are everywhere.

Travel and Other Cultures

Keep an open mind when meeting and taking in the people, culture, food, nature, animals, and ethnic and spiritual traditions when you travel.

Music has always been the greatest way to bring people of all backgrounds together with respect to each other's cultures and differences. It is a perfect opportunity to connect as human beings, enter into newfound collaborations, and enrich and advance our own humanity and art.

Internal Health

Check out some internal modes of healing or ways of balancing out your inner self. External and internal martial arts, weight-lifting, yoga, meditation, T'ai chi ch'uan and Qigong can be great art forms to practice for bringing together the mind, body and spirit.

These practices are great for facilitating the meditative zen state we fall into when we perform, and they also put us in touch with our breath and the ability to relax when we perform. We cannot have a free-flowing creative energy, nor can we be effective playing our instruments if we are not very relaxed.

Instrument & Equipment. The Machine

Here we spoke about the importance of the instruments and equipment that we acquire, and some of the variables that go along with utilizing these tools. It is ultimately all about our own self-expression in the music. In the end, the music is all anyone, including us, will care about, so we can keep the focus off the tools of the trade, and more on the music taking place.

Afterword

Music as an art form is discovered and reflected from within us and outward into the world, and has the ability to deeply influence numerous aspects of life on many fronts. In turn, the creation of music is affected by, and predisposed to, the political, ecological, sociological and cultural systems of the planet. As we tune into all this over time, we learn to see how we feel and are moved by the changes and evolutionary patterns of the earth and its people, and how that in many respects guides our direction and choices in our music and art.

So in closing, we see that there can be a lot more to developing our own sound and musical identity than just improving our instrumental, compositional, or vocal abilities, training our ear, and having great chops.

There is another instrument involved before we ever emit anything outward through our voices or external instruments. This other instrument or vessel is you. You are in touch with playing yourself first, which then goes through the voice or external instrument. The instrument is just a conduit for your conceptual output so the source of your authentic voice and sound can be channelled through into the music and outward to the listener.

Song Title Discography

Song	Artist	Recording	Label
Adagio	Jim Robitaille Group	To Music	Whaling City Sound
Adagio	Rick Frank	Brookline Summer	Decker Creek Records
Back To Bayeux	Trine	+1	Trine Arc
Lost And Found	Jim Robitaille Group	To Music	Whaling City Sound
*Yesterdays	Jim Robitaille Group	To Music	Whaling City Sound
Figures	Trine	Politics	Fuller Street Music
Arthur C.	Jim Robitaille Group	To Music	Whaling City Sound

Visit www.jimrobitaille.com/store to purchase the optional MP3 audio and score files for the five original composition, arranging, and other art form examples in Sound Origins. The PDF Ebook version of Sound Origins with audio and score files is also available at www.jimrobitaille.com/store

Visit www.jimrobitaille.com to join the mailing list and receive the latest updates on shows, recordings, and lessons.

About The Author

Guitarist and award winning composer, Jim Robitaille, has performed internationally as a sideman and a leader of his own groups. His television and live performances include: The BET Jazz Channel, The Time Warner Music Choice Jazz Channel, PBS Television, The Baird Auditorium at the Smithsonian Institute, Washington, D.C, The Bearsville Theatre, Woodstock, N.Y, The Wang Center, Boston, MA, The Knitting Factory and Smoke in New York. and internationally tours.

Jim has performed and or recorded and shared the bill with Dave Liebman, Karl Berger, Bob Moses, Gerry Gibbs, Santi Debriano, Julian Lage, Esperanza Spalding, Oscar Stagnaro, Kate McGarry, Joe Beck, the Dizzy Gillespie Alumni All-Stars, and has appeared on over 20 recordings as a leader and sideman. Awards include The 9th Annual Thelonious Monk International Jazz Composers Competition sponsored by BMI, The 2002 Great American Song Contest, The U.S.A Songwriting Competition, and The Julius Hemphill Jazz Composers Alliance Competition.

Jim is an international clinician, and a lecturer, ensemble director, and founder and director of the Performance Jam Session Series on the jazz faculty at the University of Massachusetts Dartmouth.

www.ingramcontent.com/pod-product-compliance
Lightning Source LLC
Chambersburg PA
CBHW080415170426
43194CB00015B/2823